POETRY PLUS

Intermediate

**By
Sally Fisk**

**Cover Artist
Kristina VanOss**

**Inside Illustrations by
Don O'Connor**

Published by Instructional Fair • TS Denison
an imprint of

 **McGraw-Hill
Children's Publishing**

About the Author

Sally Fisk, an elementary teacher in St. Louis County, Missouri, with over thirty years of classroom experience, received her undergraduate degree from Washburn University. She earned a Master of Arts in Teaching from Webster University. Sally has written a variety of educational materials including science, social studies, mathematics, reading comprehension, creative writing, and grammar books for grades one through six.

Credits

Author: Sally Fisk
Cover Art: Kristina VanOss
Cover Design: Annette Hollister-Papp
Inside Illustrations: Don O'Connor
Project Director/Editor: Sharon Kirkwood
Editors: Lisa Hancock, Elizabeth Flikkema
Typesetting/Layout: Lori Kibbey

McGraw-Hill
Children's Publishing

A Division of The **McGraw·Hill** Companies

Published by Instructional Fair • TS Denison
An imprint of McGraw-Hill Children's Publishing
Copyright © 1996 McGraw-Hill Children's Publishing

Send all inquiries to:
McGraw-Hill Children's Publishing
3195 Wilson Drive NW
Grand Rapids, Michigan 49544

Poetry Plus—Intermediate
ISBN: 1-56822-280-7
2 3 4 5 6 7 8 9 PHXBK 07 06 05 04 03

Table of Contents

Introduction

The purpose of *Poetry Plus* is to share with you, the classroom teacher, the joy of teaching students in the intermediate grades to write poetry. As you are well aware, trying to get students to write complete sentences is sometimes a struggle. Writing paragraphs, reports, and stories overwhelms some students. That is why teaching students to write poetry is so rewarding—they can succeed! Freed from the constraints of sentence structure, poets can experiment with rhythm and rhyming patterns, styles, and formats. Poetry allows students flexibility.

Students will learn: auditory techniques such as alliteration, and onomatopoeia; visual techniques such as diamante and pyramid poems; forms of poetry such as haiku, cinquain, and clerihew; and figures of speech such as simile and hyperbole. Students will learn that their feelings and how they express them are important. Most importantly, students will come to appreciate that reading, writing, and listening to poetry are part of a lifelong celebration of personal expression.

Poetry Plus provides all the tools you will need to turn reluctant writers into poets with pizzazz. Each lesson uses the writing process, plus an activity page for students to share, display, or publish their poetry. The lesson plan states the skills presented or reinforced and provides a list of resources and materials. Prewriting activities stimulate creative expression. The postwriting activity is a way to let students know that what they write is important enough to share. Evaluation guidelines and suggestions for extending the writing lesson are also included.

Poetry Plus begins with a *Student Self-Assessment*, a checklist that gives students responsibility for the quality of their own work. Also provided is a bulletin board idea, complete with patterns, for displaying student poems throughout the school year. A bibliography can be found on the final page of Poetry Plus.

Try to find time each day to read poetry. Even those lost minutes waiting in line can be filled with the recitation of a beautiful poem. Read with enthusiasm and expression. Experiment with choral reading. Some students may want to memorize poems. Record poems for the listening center. Provide materials in the writing center to publish poems.

The poems used for modeling in this book were written by the author, Sally Fisk.

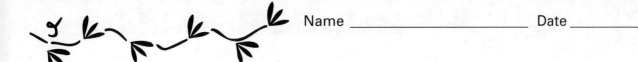

Name _____ Date _____

Student Self-Assessment

Poem title: _____

Place a check on the line as you complete each step.

_____ I participated in the prewriting activity.

_____ I followed the pattern for my poem.

_____ I participated in the response group.

_____ I checked for capitalization.

_____ I used correct punctuation.

_____ I made a neat, final copy of my poem.

_____ _____

_____ _____

Circle the word(s) that best describe(s) your feelings.

I liked this poetry lesson ...

              a lot   some   not much

I feel that I am improving my writing...

              a lot   some   not much

Tell how you might use this form of poetry again.

_____

- -

Teacher: Complete the final two steps in the rubric above by adding specific expectations as needed for each poetry lesson. Student places a check on the line as he/she completes each requirement.

Bulletin Board Idea

Directions: Cover the bulletin board with blue paper. Cut out red letters which spell *It's Rhyme Time* and attach them across the top of the bulletin board. Use tagboard to make several large watch face and/or clock patterns (page 7). Have each student trace and cut out a template of the watch face or clock on white construction paper. The student uses crayons, markers, or colored construction paper to decorate the clock or watch. Staple the students' clocks and watches to the bulletin board. Then, each student copies a poem from a favorite poet on an index card and staples it near his/her clock or watch. Encourage the students to change the poems often and to also post copies of their own poems.

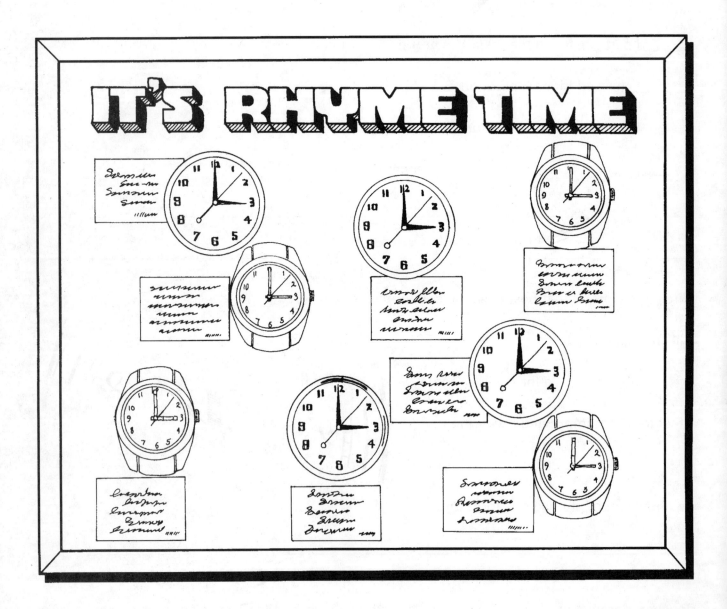

Bulletin Board Patterns

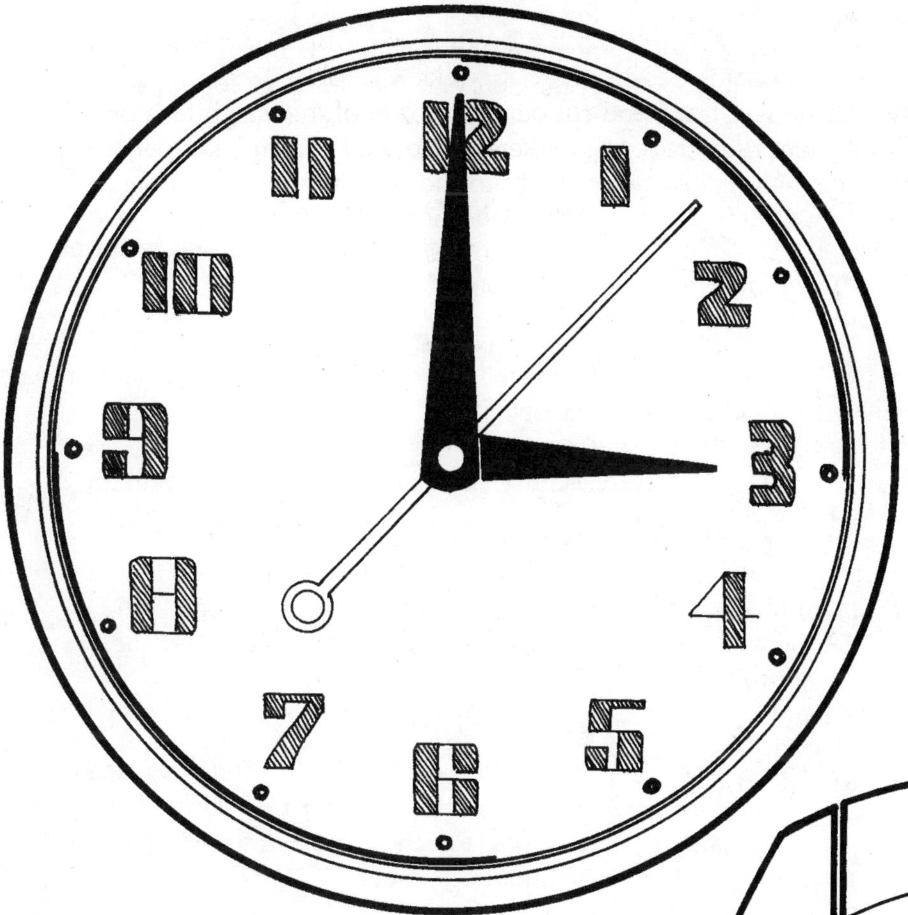

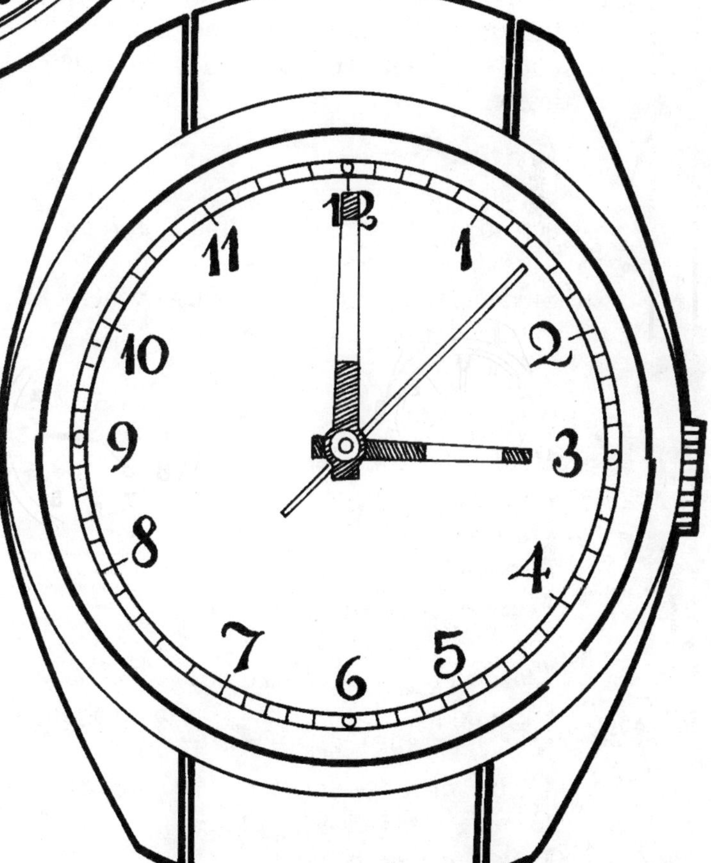

Acrostic

Developing Skills
Students will write acrostic poems about Abraham Lincoln.

Resources/Materials
Resources: reference books, magazine articles, and nonfiction books about Abraham Lincoln such as Lee Morgan's *Abraham Lincoln*, Lloyd Ostendorf's *Abraham Lincoln: The Boy, The Man*, and Augusta Stevenson's *Abraham Lincoln: The Great Emancipator*.

Materials: copies of the activity page, chart paper, markers, paper, pencils, construction paper, scissors, and glue

Prewriting
Use this writing lesson during February, Presidents' Month. Allow children time to read books and articles about Abraham Lincoln. They should keep notes on file cards. Then, ask them to contribute facts they discovered about his childhood. Write them on chart paper. Next, ask them to help make another chart about Lincoln's adult life. Keep these charts for the writing lesson.

Writing
Explain that each student will create an acrostic poem using the name *Abraham Lincoln* and phrases related to him. Students will use the information generated on the class charts. Share the example.

Admired by many Americans
Born in Kentucky in 1809
Real sense of humor
Abe was his nickname
Honest and kind
Attorney in Springfield, Illinois
Married Mary Todd in 1842

Lived in a log cabin as a boy
Inspired people with the Gettysburg address
Nancy Hanks Lincoln was his mother
Civil War president from 1861 to 1865
Older sister was Sarah Lincoln
Loved to read books
New Salem was his home as a young man

Responding
Each student shares his/her acrostic with a response team. Students make favorable comments and suggest ideas for improving the poems. Peers check that the information about Lincoln is accurate.

Revising/Editing
Authors make any corrections and revisions needed and check capitalization.

Postwriting
Each student makes a neat copy of his/her acrostic. Then, he/she makes a "peeper" following the directions on the activity page. Use the "peeper" to display the poem.

Evaluating
The student used the correct form and accurate information for the poem. The student made a "peeper" to display the poem.

Extending Writing
During Presidents' Month, students research information about other presidents to write acrostics. Put the poems in a class book in chronological order.

Abraham Lincoln *(acrostic)*

Follow the steps to make a "peeper."

2. Trace and cut out face pattern on manila drawing papers. Add facial features with crayons or markers.(See sketch of completed "peeper.")

1. Trace and cut out the hat pattern on black construction paper. Keep the pattern for step two.

3. Trace and cut out the beard pattern on the fold of black construction paper. Glue it on the face as shown. Next, glue the hat.

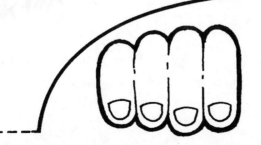

4. Trace and cut out the hand pattern on manila drawing paper. Make two. Draw in the fingernails. Glue on hand on either side of the head as shown.

5. Make a neat copy of your acrostic poem to hang below the "peeper."

Alliteration

Developing Skills
Students will use the poetic device of alliteration to write tongue twisters.

Resource/Materials
Resources: *Alvin Schwartz's Twister of Twists, A Tangler of Tongues* and Charles Keller's *Tongue Twisters.*

Materials: chart paper, markers, several colors of construction paper, glue, and scissors

Prewriting
Ask students if they are familiar with any tongue twisters. Write several examples on a chart. Explain that most of the words in a tongue twister have the same beginning sound. Underline those words. Then, write this example on chart paper.

> *Freddy freaked out Friday when Frank fried frankfurters.*

Choose a letter of the alphabet that is not the same as any student's name. Have students contribute words that begin with that letter to create a class tongue twister. Underline the examples of alliteration.

Writing
At the next session have students write tongue twisters using their own names with words that have the same beginning sound.

Responding
In response groups, each student has the opportunity to share his/her tongue twister. The other students suggest improvements or additions to the poems.

Revising/Editing
Authors make revisions and edit their poems. They can try different formats for their poems.

Examples:
> *Freddy*
> *freaked out*
> > *Friday when*
> > > *Frank*
> > *fried*
> *frankfurters.*

> *Freddy freaked out*
> *Friday when*
> *Frank*
> *fried*
> *frankfurters.*

Postwriting
Students make a final copy of their poem on the tongue of the alien faces created by following the directions on the activity page.

Evaluating
The student used alliteration to write a tongue twister and followed directions to create alien faces.

Extending Writing
Write tongue twisters about zoo animals for a class book called *Aardvark to Zebra: Tongue Twisters about Zoo Animals.*

Example:
> *Camilla Camel*
> *caught cold while*
> *carefully carrying*
> *colorful carnations.*

Write tongue twisters about food when studying a unit about nutrition.

Example:
> *Paula and Pete*
> *proudly popped popcorn*
> *in the popcorn popper.*

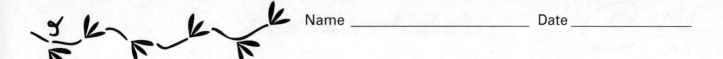

Name _____ Date _____

Alien Tongue Twisters *(alliteration)*

To create an alien tongue twister:

1. On a 9" x 12" sheet of colored construction paper, draw an outline of an alien face with black marker. Cut outside the black line.

2. Cut or tear facial features (eyes, ears, nose, mouth, hair) from different colors of construction paper. Glue onto the face.

3. Enlarge the pattern below, or cut a 1½" x 12" strip out of construction-paper for a tongue.

4. Write your tongue twister poem on the tongue.

5. Wrap the tongue around a pencil to make it curl. Remove the pencil and attach the back of the tongue to the alien's mouth.

6. Display on the classroom or hallway bulletin board where others may read your tongue twister.

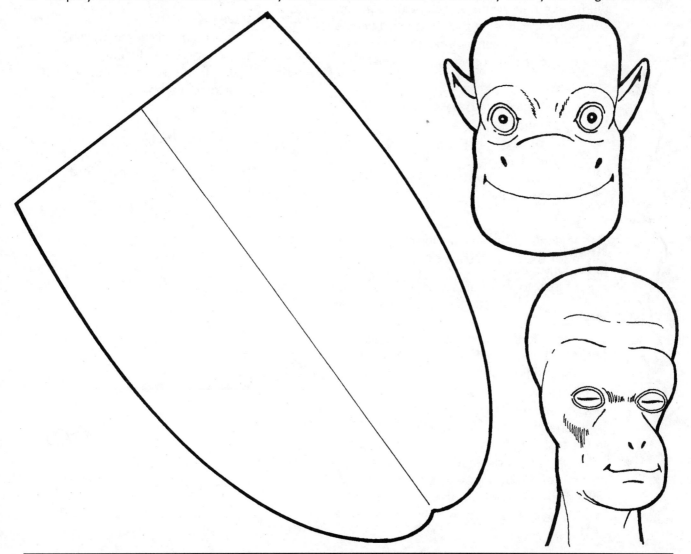

Alphabet Poem

Developing Skills
Students will use dictionary skills and alliteration to write an alphabet poem. The words in the poem relate to the poem topic.

Materials
Materials: copies of the activity page, dictionaries, paper, pencils, glue, construction paper, markers, and scissors

Prewriting
Write this list of words on a chart or the chalkboard: elephant, eat, enormous, ear, earth, elegant, endanger, enjoy, entertain, excite, every. Ask students if they notice anything unusual about the list. (Every word begins with e.) Then, explain that you are going to use some of these words to write an alphabet poem about an elephant. Select words that refer to the subject, elephants, in some way. Make sure that an e word begins each line. Write your own poem or use the example. Each line begins with a capital letter.

Elephants

Elephants have
Enormous
Ears and
Elegant ivory tusks. They
Excite and
Entertain us at the circus.

Ask students to think of a subject for a poem for the next class session. (You may want to choose a category such as *animals* for the students to consider.)

Writing
During the next period, have each student use the dictionary to make a list of words that could relate to his/her chosen topic. Words must begin with the same beginning letter as the topic. Then, instruct students to begin their poems by mentioning the subject in the first line. Each line that follows must begin with the same letter. However, students can add other words and other endings to the words on their list. Poems should be about five or six lines.

Responding
In a small peer group, each student shares his/her original list of words and rough draft of his/her poem. The group makes positive statements about the chosen words. Students make suggestions for substituting or adding other words from a student's word list to the poem.

Revising/Editing
Each student makes revisions and meets again with the response group. Students check each other's poems to make sure the poem follows the correct format.

Postwriting
Each student copies his/her poem on the sides of a box made by following the directions on the activity page.

Evaluating
The student used the dictionary to find appropriate words. The student chose words relating to his/her poem topic. The student constructed a box on which to display his/her poem.

Extending Writing
Write a class poem instead of individual poems. Students can contribute words to the list and make suggestions for how to use the words in the poem. The teacher will ensure that the poem follows the correct form.

Pairs of students can work together to write a poem about a unit of study.

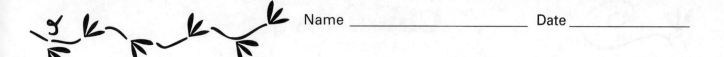

Elephant *(alphabet poem)*

Follow the directions to make the box for the poem "Elephants." Then, repeat the directions to make a box for your poem.

1. Cut a 9" x 9" square of construction paper.

2. Fold the paper in thirds in two directions, creating nine squares. Cut slits as shown in the illustration.

3. Use markers or crayons to draw a picture about the subject of your poem in the center square.

4. Write the title of your poem and the first line in the center square of one side.

5. Then, write the other lines of your poem in the center squares of each of the other three sides.

6. Fold and glue the tabs to form a box.

tab **A**		tab **C**
Glue tab A to tab B. Then glue the center square on top.	Elegant ivory tusks. They	Glue tab C to tab D. Then glue the center square on top.
Excite and Entertain us at the circus.	*[elephant illustration]*	Enormous Ears and
tab **B**	**Elephants** Elephants have	tab **D**

TAB A
TAB B

TAB A
TAB B

FOLD DOWN AND GLUE
TAB A

Cinquain

Developing Skills
Students will use nouns, adjectives, and verbs to write cinquains about Plains Indians.

Resources/Materials
Resources: Maria Campbell's *People of the Buffalo*, Rae Bains' *Indians of the Plains*, and Keith Brandt's *Indian Homes and Indian Crafts*

Materials for each student: copy of the activity page, bag, markers, cellophane tape, scissors, a rubber band, and four 10-inch sticks or four flexible drinking straws

Prewriting
Brainstorm and record on chart paper information learned from the students' study of the Plains Indians.

Writing
Write the cinquain pattern on chart paper or the chalkboard. Explain any unfamiliar terms. Instruct each student to choose a specific tribe of Plains Indians to write about. Examples: *Arapaho, Blackfeet, Cheyenne, Comanche, Crow, Kiowa, Osage, Pawnee*, and *Sioux*.

Pattern:
Line 1: noun
Line 2: two adjectives describing the noun
Line 3: three verbs showing action of the
       noun
Line 4: four-word statement telling about the
       noun
Line 5: repeat the noun or use a synonym
       for the noun

Example:
  Cheyenne
  Skilled, brave
  Hunted, fished, farmed
  They lived in tepees
  Shahiyena ("People of Strange Speech")

Responding
Students meet in groups to share their poems. Members of the groups make favorable comments about the poems. They check that line two contains adjectives and line three contains verbs.

Revising/Editing
Each author makes changes, if desired. He/she checks the poem for punctuation, capitalization, and adherence to the cinquain pattern.

Postwriting
The student follows directions on the activity page to construct an Indian tepee. The author copies his/her cinquain directly onto brown paper with markers.

Evaluating
The student followed the pattern of the cinquain to write a poem using his/her knowledge of Plains Indians. The student made a neat copy of his/her cinquain on the tepee.

Extending Writing
Instruct each student to write a paragraph from an Indian's point of view describing a buffalo hunt.

Have children construct a Plains Indian village with the tepees they made.

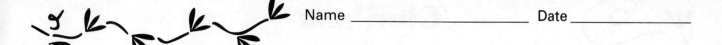

Tepee *(cinquain)*

1. Cut out the tepee pattern.

2. Cut a large section from a brown paper grocery bag. Wad and unwad the paper until it is soft and crinkled. This piece of paper represents a buffalo hide.

3. Fold the piece of "hide." Trace the tepee pattern on the brown paper. Cut it out.

4. Using markers, write your cinquain about Plains Indians in the center of the tepee. Decorate the tepee with Indian designs.

5. Cross the four sticks or straws and secure them with a rubber band.

6. Wrap the tepee "hide" around the four "poles." Cross the top points and tape.

7. Tape the two edges of the "hide" to two of the "poles," making an opening into the tepee. Adjust the "poles" until the tepee is free-standing.

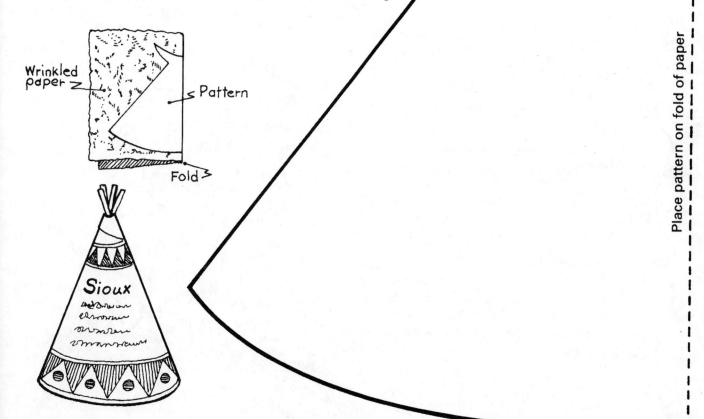

Place pattern on fold of paper

Clerihew

Developing Skills
Students will use rhyme to write a four-lined humorous poem.

Materials
Materials: copies of the activity page, chart paper, markers, writing paper, and pencils. (Materials for the doll include tagboard, crayons, cloth scraps, wallpaper pieces, construction paper, ribbon, buttons, yarn, and hole punch.)

Prewriting
Explain to the class that a clerihew is a four-lined humorous poem about a person, real or fictitious. It was originated by Edmund *Clerihew* Bentley (1875–1956), a British writer. The poem follows a pattern. Write the pattern and the two examples on a chart.

Pattern
Line 1 ends with a person's name.
Line 2 rhymes with line 1.
Lines 3 and 4 rhyme with each other.

Examples:
My friend Lou
Lost his tennis shoe.
Now that he has just one,
His worries have begun.

My friend Jill
went up the hill.
I think she met Jack,
'cause she never came back!

Writing
Each student writes a clerihew about a friend or a character from a story or poem.

Responding
Students meet in response groups to share their clerihews. Students make positive comments about the poems. They check the rhyming pattern and give suggestions for improvements.

Revising/Editing
Authors make necessary corrections. They check for capitalization and punctuation.

Postwriting
Each student makes a copy of his/her clerihew for a class book. Then, he/she follows the directions on the activity page to make a cube on which to publish the poem.

Evaluating
The writer followed the rhyming pattern to produce a clerihew. The student contributed a neat copy of his/her poem for a class book. The student made a cube to display the poem.

Extending Writing
Write clerihews for family members' birthdays, Mother's Day, or Father's Day. Illustrate a greeting card and write the clerihew inside.

Jack and Jill *(clerihew)*

Cut out the pattern below. Trace it on tagboard and cut out. Write your clerihew on one side. Use cloth scraps, wallpaper pieces, construction paper, ribbon, buttons, etc., to "dress" the other side of the doll to look like the character in your poem. Use yarn for hair. Add features with crayons or markers. Use a hole punch to punch a hole in the top of the head. Thread a length of yarn or ribbon through the hole and hang the doll so both sides are visible.

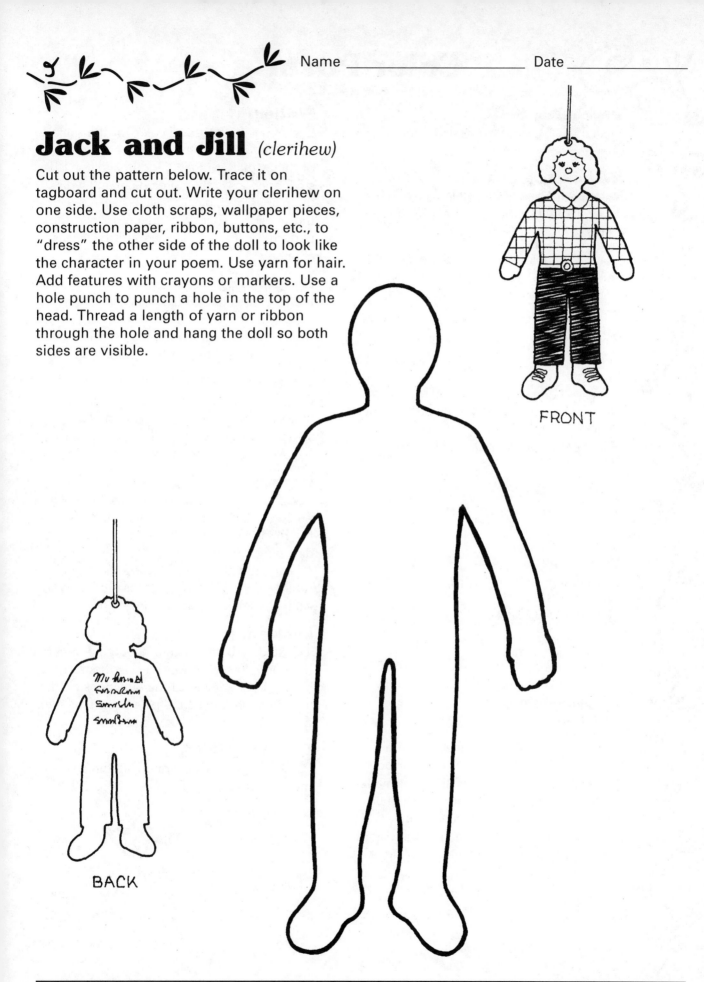

FRONT

BACK

Color Poem

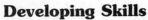

Developing Skills
Students will use rhyme to write poems about color.

Resources/Materials
Resources: *The Random House Book of Poetry for Children*, edited by Jack Prelutsky

Materials: copies of the activity page, chart paper, markers, writing paper, tagboard, old magazines, scissors, glue, pencils, and laminating materials

Prewriting
Read David McCord's "Yellow," Christina Rossetti's "What Is Pink?" and Mary O'Neill's "What is Red?" from *The Random House Book of Poetry for Children*. Then, on a chart, write the example of the poem below patterned after David McCord's poem "Yellow."

Example:

White

Bushes are green,
Red is a rose;
White is the color
The winter wind blows.

Buttercups are yellow
Blue is the sky;
White is ice cream
Atop apple pie.

Purple's for kings,
Pink is for lace;
White is the snowflake
That lands on my face.

Explain that the poem has an *abcb* rhyming pattern (the second and fourth lines rhyme). Lines one and two name colors other than the title color. Line three names the color in the title and line four rhymes with line two.

Writing
Each student chooses a color for the subject of his/her poem. Next, he/she makes a list of things that are that color. In addition, the student chooses six more colors and writes the names of things usually associated with those colors. Then, the student follows the pattern for the poem to write three verses about a color.

Responding
If a student is having difficulty thinking of specific items for different colors, the response team can make suggestions. They should listen for the abcb rhyming pattern.

Revising/Editing
Each student makes his/her revisions so that the poem follows the pattern. The student should check for the correct usage of capitals and punctuation.

Postwriting
The student makes a copy of his/her color poem for a class booklet called "Colors of the Rainbow." Then, the student follows the directions on the activity page to make a palette on which to display another copy of his/her poem. You may choose to laminate each student's work when finished.

Evaluating
The student contributed a neat copy of his/her color poem for the class booklet. Then, he/she followed the directions on the activity page to create a palette on which to display another copy of the poem.

Extending Writing
Paint a picture incorporating all the colors mentioned in the poem.

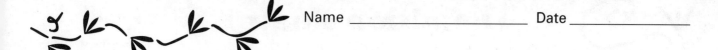

Name _____ Date _____

Artist's Palette *(color poem)*

To make a palette:

1. Cut out and trace the palette pattern on a piece of 8½" x 11" tagboard.

2. Cut out the tagboard palette.

3. Cut pictures from old magazines showing things that match the color in the tile of your poem.

4. Glue the pictures on the palette, creating a collage.

5. Then, glue a copy of your poem in the center of the palette.

**Cut
Out**

Definition Poetry

Developing Skills

Students will use commas in a series and both capitals and question marks appropriately. Students will use their knowledge of the United States Constitution to write a poem.

Resources/Materials

Resources: reference materials about the Constitution, social studies textbooks, pictures of the signing of the Constitution such as Howard Chandler Christy's painting.

Materials: copies of the activity page, chart paper, markers, paper, pencils, pen and ink (or fine-line black markers), two 10" dowel rods per student, and tape

Prewriting

Use this lesson after studying about the Constitution of the United States. Have a member of the class read the Preamble to the Constitution of the United States. Then, have the class brainstorm facts they learned during the unit of study. Record the facts on a chart to keep for the next class session.

Writing

During the next session, write the first two lines of the following example poem on the board. Explain that the students will add phrases to complete the second line, using facts brainstormed at the previous session. Instruct them to indent the phrases and begin each on a new line. Suggest that each student write at least four or five phrases. The last line, "That's the Constitution," is flush left.

For aiding reluctant writers, write the entire example poem on a chart for a guide. Have students work together to write a group poem, if necessary.

The Constitution

What is The Constitution of the United States?
The Constitution…
  replaced the Articles of Confederation,
  was written in 1787 in Philadelphia,
  is the supreme law of the land,
  has a preamble, seven articles, and
    twenty-six amendments,
  divides the government into three
    branches,
  includes The Bill of Rights,
  defines the duties and powers of the
    Congress, the President, and the
    Supreme Court.
That's the Constitution!

Responding

Students meet in response groups to share their poems. Students make positive comments about another's work. The members of the group may challenge the accuracy of facts.

Revising/Editing

Each author makes necessary revisions to have accurate information about the Constitution. The author checks the form of his/her poem.

Postwriting

Each student copies his/her poem on the activity page in pen and ink or uses fine-line black markers.

Evaluating

The student used his/her knowledge about the Constitution of the United States to write a definition poem. The student reproduced the poem in pen and ink on the activity page.

Extending Writing

Have students write definition poems for:

What is Congress?

Who was James Madison?

What is The Bill of Rights?

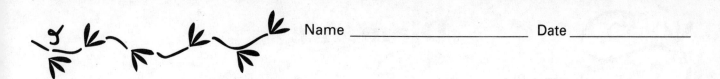

The Constitution *(definition poetry)*

To make a scroll:

1. Write your poem on the scroll with pen and ink (or a fine-tip marking pen).

2. Cut out the scroll and attach it to two small dowels.

We the People

Diamante

Developing Skills

Students will contrast two topics, following the form for a diamante poem. Students will use nouns, adjectives, and participles.

Resource/Materials

Resource: *The Random House Book of Poetry for Children*, edited by Jack Prelutsky.

Materials: copies of the activity page, two 10" white paper plates per student, glue, scissors, chart paper, markers, writing paper, pencils, and ribbon

Prewriting

Read several selections from *The Random House Book of Poetry for Children* about city life such as Marci Ridlon's "City, City," Jack Prelutsky's "City, Oh City," Langston Hughes' "City Lights," and Lois Lenski's "Sing a Song of People." Then, share some poems about country life.

Writing

At the next class session, have each student write *City* in the center of the top line of his/her paper. Brainstorm and list adjectives on a chart that describe the city. The student chooses two of them for the second line. Then, record the students' suggestions for -ing words that relate to the city. Each student writes three participles centered on the third line. The fourth line should begin with two nouns that relate to the city. Save the papers.

At the next writing session, brainstorm nouns, participles, and adjectives relating to country life. Return student papers from the previous session. Students begin on line four and write two nouns relating to the country. Line five lists three *-ing* words. Line six has two adjectives and line seven has the word Country.

Diamante Pattern

one noun
two adjectives
three participles
two nouns/two nouns
three participles
two adjectives
one noun

Example:

City vs. Country

City
Big, busy
Hustling, bustling, hurrying
Skyscrapers, factories, barns, meadows,
Planting, growing, harvesting,
Quiet, green
Country

Responding

Students share their poems in peer groups. Students respond positively to the poems and make suggestions for improving them.

Revising/Editing

Authors make any necessary revisions. They meet in response groups again to check each other's poems to make sure the pattern has been followed.

Postwriting

Students copy their poems on copies of the activity page. Then, following the directions, they make the city and country wall hanging.

Evaluating

The student compares city life and country life with appropriate vocabulary in a diamante poem.

Extending Writing

Have students compare night and day, youth and age, or two characters from a story in a diamante poem.

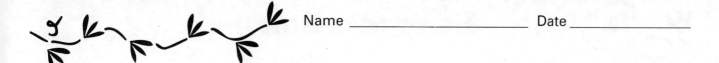
City vs. Country *(diamante)*

To make a wall hanging: Copy your diamante poem on the writing lines at the bottom of the page. Cut out the diamond shape and glue it on a piece of construction paper cut 1/2" larger than the diamond. Allow it to dry.

1. Draw a line across the center of one 10" white paper plate.

2. Using crayons or markers, draw a picture of a city scene on the top half of the plate and a country scene on the bottom half of the plate.

3. Cut out the center on a second 10" white paper plate, leaving the fluted rim whole.

4. Turn the rim upside-down and glue it onto the rim of the plate with the pictures. You will see the pictures through the frame.

5. After the plates are sealed and the glue is dry, attach the plates to a length of ribbon with a bow at the top and the diamond-shaped paper with the poem below to create a wall hanging.

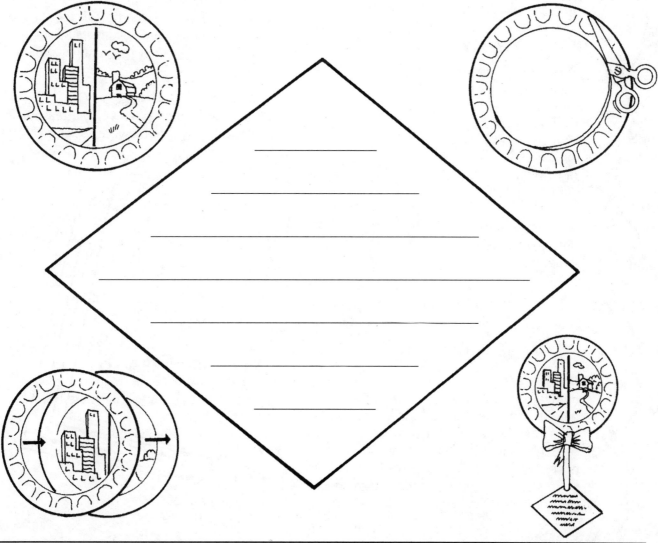

Exaggeration

Developing Skills
Students will become familiar with hyperbole and write couplets in exaggeration poems. Students will use question marks appropriately.

Materials
Materials: copies of the activity page, chart paper, markers, paper, and pencils

Prewriting
Explain that hyperbole is exaggeration, not to be taken literally. Ask if anyone knows a "fish story." Ask why someone might want to tell a big lie. The class will then have an opportunity to use their imaginations to write couplets for exaggeration poems. Write the example on chart paper and ask why each couplet, except the last, is an example of hyperbole.

Example:
Did You Hear?

Did you hear about
The hundred-pound trout?

The honeybee
That can ski?

The unicorn
That blows a horn?

The dinosaur
That lives next door?

The little pig
That can dance a jig?

It must be true.
I heard it from you!

Writing
Students write couplets, following the pattern. The first line and the last couplet should be the same as the example. Students may find it easier to write hyperbole if they choose topics for their poems such as: sports figures, movie stars, cartoon characters, animals, and so on.

Responding
Peers listen as each student reads his/her poem aloud. They comment on the couplets they particularly like. They make suggestions to the author for improving the poem.

Revising/Editing
Authors make revisions and return to the response groups for final checks on capitalization and correct usage of question marks.

Postwriting
Each student follows directions on the activity page to make an accordion booklet. Then, the author writes his/her exaggeration poem in the booklet.

Evaluating
The student wrote hyperbole in the form of couplets. The student used question marks correctly. The student made an accordion booklet.

Extending Writing
Write exaggeration poems about reasons for not completing a homework assignment.

Did You Hear? *(exaggeration)*

To make an accordion book:
1. Cut out the two strips.
2. Join the two strips at the tab with a piece of cellophane tape.
3. Write a different verse of your exaggeration poem on each page.

4. Illustrate each page.
5. Accordion fold the booklet on the dotted lines.
6. Write the title "Did You Hear?" on the front cover.

Tab

Haiku

Developing Skills
Students will learn the form of haiku poetry. They will learn syllabication. Students will make an origami water bird.

Materials
Materials: chalkboard and chalk, writing paper and pencils, and very light-weight typing paper

Prewriting
Use this lesson as a culminating activity for a unit on water fowl or autumn. Explain that haiku is an ancient form of Japanese poetry that is most often about nature. The poems follow a particular syllabic pattern.

Writing
Explain that haiku is a three-line unrhymed poem with a special pattern: lines one and three have five syllables, and line two has seven syllables. Write the examples of haiku on the board and mark each syllable. Students choose water fowl to write about: ducks, geese, swans, and so on.

Example:

Flying in a V,
The Canada geese head south.
Winter is coming!

Autumn's in the air.
The snow geese honk overhead
On their long journey.

Near the shallow pond,
Fluffy yellow ducks waddle
Behind their mother.

A silent swimmer,
The beautiful white swan looks
At its reflection.

Responding
Students share their haiku with their response groups. Members make positive comments and suggestions for improvements.

Revising/Editing
The author makes changes to improve his/her poem. Then, the peer groups check each other's poems for the correct syllabic patterns.

Postwriting
Each student makes a final copy of his/her poem. Then, the student makes an origami water bird following the directions on the activity page.

Evaluating
The student wrote a three-line poem following the haiku pattern. The student produced a legible copy of the poem. The student made an origami water bird.

Extending Writing
Study Japanese culture, history, and people. Write a report about a favorite topic.

Waterfowl *(haiku)*

To make an origami waterfowl:

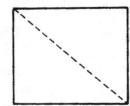

1. Fold an 8½" square of thin typing paper in half diagonally. Open.

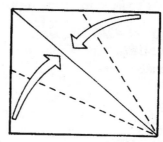

2. Fold each side to the center fold.

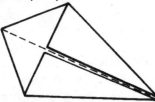

3. Fold the paper in half again at the center fold.

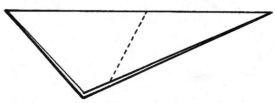

4. Beginning about 4½" from the narrow end, fold the top half to the center. Crease and unfold. Do the same with the bottom half. (Note: You can make the body more like a duck's by increasing the distance you make the fold from the narrow end.)

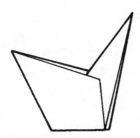

5. Open and reverse the fold to make the bird's neck.

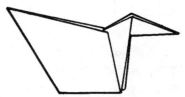

6. About 2½" from the tip of the neck, fold the top half to the center. Crease and unfold. Do the same with the bottom half.

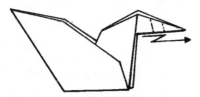

7. Open and reverse the fold to make the bird's head.

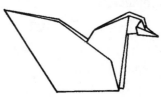

8. Make a reverse fold to form a beak.

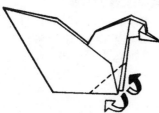

9. Fold each side up about 1" to make the bird stand.

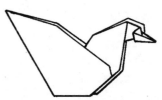

10. Copy the haiku on one side of the bird.

Initial Poetry

Developing Skills
Students use picturesque phrases from various sources to create a poem.

Resources/Materials
Resources: poetry books and storybooks

Materials: copies of the activity page, crayons, glue, scissors, construction paper, and markers

Prewriting
Write your initials on the board, leaving a large space between each letter. Then, read aloud poems that have particularly picturesque phrases. Ask students to recall any phrases that begin with one of your initials. Be prepared to locate some in the poems you have read. Make a list of at least three phrases for each initial. The phrases need not be related.

Example:

E	**S**
evening breezes	*summer's frolicking*
endless sky	*stately trees*
emerald green	*song-singing thrush*

R
rustling leaves
raindrops splashing
river racing

Then, combine one phrase from each list to form an initial poem.

Examples:

Emerald green,
Stately trees bow to the
River racing by.

Evening breezes,
Summer's frolicking in the
Rustling leaves.

Writing
Allow students time to search for picturesque phrases in poetry books and storybooks. They should add to their lists as they locate new phrases. (Consider giving this as a homework assignment.)

At the next writing period, demonstrate again how to list the phrases under the initials. If two people have an identical initial, encourage these students to share lists. Then, check the lists to make sure the phrases do begin with the correct initials.

At the next session, have the students experiment with combining one phrase from each column to make a poem. One strategy is to write each phrase on a slip of paper. Then, students can move phrases about until a pleasing poem is formed. (Keep the original lists, in case lines need revising later.)

Responding
Peers listen as each student reads his/her poem aloud. Then they comment on the lines they particularly like. They can make suggestions to the author of how to improve the poem.

Revising/Editing
Each student revises his/her own poem and returns to the response group to share the revisions. Students check for proper usage of spelling, capitalization, and punctuation.

Postwriting
Each student creates a pattern with his/her initials, following the directions on the activity page. Then, he/she copies the initial poem on the inside of the card with colored markers.

Evaluating
The student wrote an initial poem using picturesque phrases from outside sources. The student made an initial pattern and printed his/her poem on the inside of the card.

Extending Writing
Encourage students to keep a list of phrases as they find them in their recreational reading. Then, they can write initial poems for family and friends.

Patterns *(initial poetry)*

To make the pattern card:

1. Choose three colors of crayons, one for each of your initials.

2. Write your initials across the top row of the grid in crayon, repeating the initials and color pattern.

3. Go to the second line when the first is filled. Continue until you reach the last square.

4. Then, create a different design for each of your three initials, using the two other colors.

5. Repeat the designs on the grid until each square is complete.

6. Trace over the grid lines with a crayon to make the squares stand out. Cut out the grid.

7. Fold a 9" x 12" piece of colored construction paper in half vertically. Glue your grid on the front.

8. On the inside, copy your initial poem in your best handwriting.

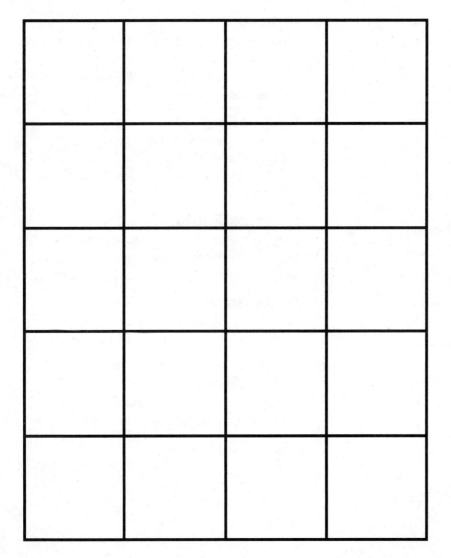

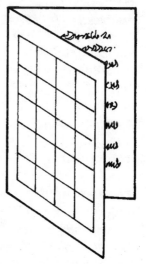

List Poems

Developing Skills
Students use lists from menus to write quatrains (four-line rhyming poems).

Resources/Materials
Resources: actual menus and copies of menus from a variety of restaurants including fast-food eateries

Materials: copies of the activity page, chart paper (or poster board), markers, writing paper, and pencils

Prewriting
Display the menus. Have enough for each student to have one or a copy of a menu. Explain that the class will generate poems from the lists of foods offered on the menus, following a prescribed pattern. Display the poems below on chart paper or poster board. They are patterned after Shel Silverstein's poem "Eighteen Flavors."

Pie in the Sky
Blackberry, boysenberry,
Blueberry, too.
Strawberry, gooseberry,
Raspberry for you.

Banana cream, Boston cream,
Chocolate cream, too.
Pumpkin cream, coconut cream,
Raisin cream for you.

Pizza Party
Sausage, green pepper,
Canadian bacon, too.
Mushroom, onion,
Mozzarella for you.

Anchovies, olives,
Pepperoni, too.
Provel, Romano,
Pizza for you.

Oriental Delight
Almond Chicken, Garlic Chicken,
Cashew Chicken, too.
Hunan Chicken, Lemon Chicken,
Broccoli Chicken for you.

Crispy Shrimp, Szechwan Shrimp,
Snowbird Shrimp, too.
Sesame Beef, Mandarin Beef,
Hot Braised Beef for you.

Just a Little Italian
Red Sauces:
Cannelloni, Manicotti,
Ravioli, too.
Lasagna, Mostaccioli,
Pasta Primavera for you.

White Sauces:
Cavatelli, Fettucine,
Linguine, too.
Rigatoni, Tortellini,
Pasta con Broccoli for you.

Writing
Students should experiment with placement of the words from the menu lists to produce rhythmical poems. Encourage them to write at least two verses.

Responding
Students meet in response groups. Each student shares his/her poem by reading it aloud. Group members make positive comments.

Revising/Editing
Authors make changes to poems that will improve them. Students check for proper usage of capitalization and punctuation.

Postwriting
The student decorates a menu cover and copies his/her list poem on the inside of the menu.

Evaluating
The student followed the quatrain pattern to produce a poem from a menu list.

Extending Writing
Use other sources of lists to generate ideas for poems. For example, use lists of names from the telephone book or items from a catalog.

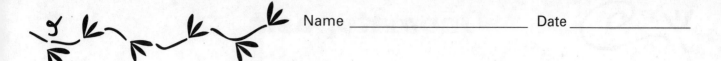
What's for Dinner? *(list poems)*

To make a menu:

1. Cut out the menu frame and fold it in half, either lengthwise or vertically.

2. Write the name of your restaurant on the cover of your menu and decorate it.

3. Copy your list poem neatly on the inside.

Onomatopoeia

Developing Skills
Students will use words that imitate sounds to write a poem. Students will use quotations and punctuate them correctly.

Resources/Materials
Resources: words and music to "Old MacDonald Had a Farm"

Materials: copies of the activity page, cereal boxes, chart paper, markers, writing paper, pencils, glue, construction paper, crayons, and scissors

Prewriting
Read the words to "Old MacDonald Had a Farm" and have the students sing it. Explain that words that imitate sounds are examples of onomatopoeic words. In this case, they relate to sounds heard on a farm. Keep a list of the words and sounds. The list need not be limited to animal sounds.
Examples:
moo—cow; quack—duck; oink—pig; neigh—horse; cluck—hen; gobble—turkey; cock-a-doodle-do—rooster; buzz—bee; hiss—snake; whoooo—owl; crunch—animals eating; va-room—truck; splash—water; chop—cutting wood; creak—barn door; clomp—animals walking; gurgle—water; whoosh—wind; bang—gun

Writing
At the next session, review the onomatopoeic words from the chart. Add any new words the students have thought of to the list, and then have students write several couplets about the sounds heard on a farm. Couplets are two lines of verse that rhyme.

Examples:

*The goat said, "Cr-unch, cr-unch.
I'm eating my lunch, my lunch."*

*The horse said, "Neigh, neigh.
I like this sweet hay."*

*"Moo, moo," said the brown cow.
"I shall give my milk now."*

*"Whoooo, whoooo," said the owl.
"I'm out on my nightly prowl."*

Responding
Students read their poems to their peer group. Students should listen closely for onomatopoeic words in each verse. Members of the group may make suggestions to improve the couplets.

Revising/Editing
Using suggestions given by the response team, authors make necessary corrections. Then, they edit their work for capitalization and punctuation, especially material within the quotations.

Postwriting
Each student makes a neat copy of his/her couplets. Then, he/she follows the directions on the activity page to make the barn.

Evaluating
The student wrote couplets, each with onomatopoeic words. The student used appropriate capitalization and punctuation. The student followed directions on the activity page to make a barn.

Extending Writing
Write a short story about life on a farm from an animal's point of view.

Collect poems about animals that use onomatopoeic words. Keep them in a scrapbook.

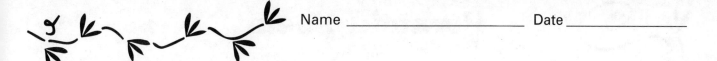

Hee-Haw *(onomatopoeia)*

To make a barn: Cover the back and sides of a cereal box with red, gray, or brown construction paper. Color and cut out the barn picture. Cut on the dotted lines to make the windows and doors of the barn open. Next, glue the barn to a piece of light-colored construction paper. (Do not glue the windows and doors.) Write a different couplet from your onomatopoeic poem behind each window and door. Then, glue the barn picture on the front of your box. Attach a copy of your entire poem to the back of the box.

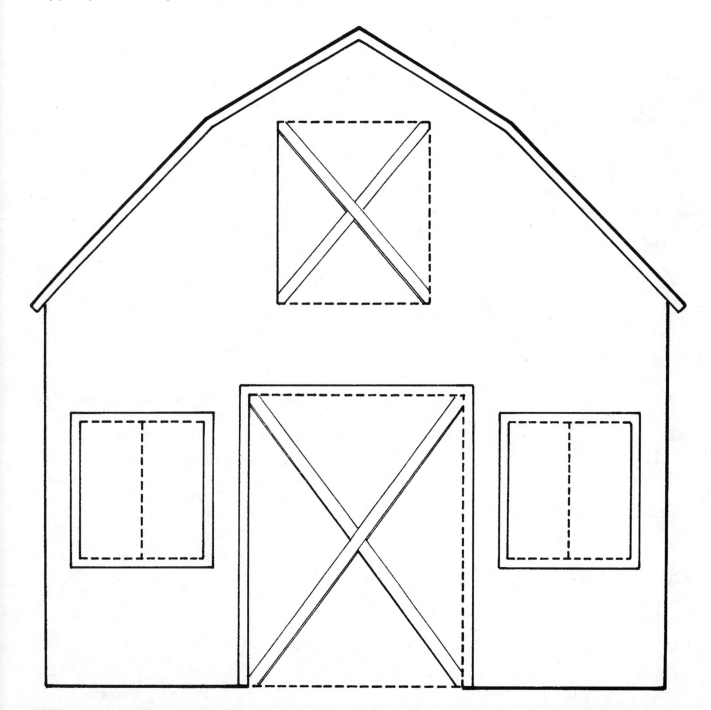

Pyramid Poem

Developing Skills

Students will use their knowledge of insects to write pyramid poems. The students will use capitals, commas, and periods correctly. Students will construct insects' habitats in which to display their poems.

Resources/Materials

Resources: reference books, fiction and non-fiction books about insects, videos, filmstrips and pictures of insects

Materials: chart paper, markers, writing paper, pencils, construction paper, and crayons

Prewriting

When studying insects, pay close attention to names of insects. Write the names on a chart. Then, write the two following poetry examples on the board. Point out that each poem contains facts about insects. Some words describe the insect's appearance. Others describe what it eats and its habitat.

Examples:

> *Bees*
> *Have stingers,*
> *Live in hives,*
> *Collect nectar from flowers,*
> *Some are drones and workers,*
> *Bees are important insects to farmers.*

> *Dragonfly*
> *Long body,*
> *Four clear wings,*
> *Eats variety of insects,*
> *Lays its eggs in water,*
> *Nymphs live in water two years.*

Instruct each student to choose a particular insect of which to make an in-depth study. The student keeps the data collected on a semantic web.

Writing

Using the information recorded on his/her web, the student follows a specific pattern to write a pyramid poem. Explain that each line is one word longer than the preceding line. Students may need to adjust spacing between letters and words to achieve the desired pyramid appearance of the poem. Encourage students to write at least five or six lines.

Responding

Students share their pyramid poems in response groups. Team members make favorable comments about the poems. They need to check that each line is one word longer than the line preceding it.

Revising/Editing

Authors make necessary revisions and check for mechanics and style.

Postwriting

Each student makes one copy of his/her poem on writing paper for a class book titled "Interesting Insects." Then, the student follows the directions on the activity page to create an insect's habitat on which to display his/her poem.

Evaluating

The student used accurate information about an insect to write a pyramid poem. The student made neat copies of his/her poem for a class book and created the three-dimensional insect habitat.

Extending Writing

With a partner, have students create a Venn diagram to compare and contrast two insects. Use information from both students' webs and pyramid poems to complete the diagram.

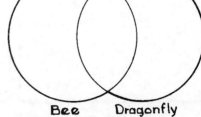

Bee   Dragonfly

Busy Bees *(pyramid poem)*

To make an insect habitat:

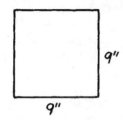

1. Cut a 9" square of drawing paper.

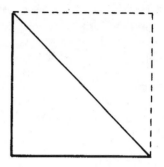

2. Fold the square diagonally. Repeat with the other corner.

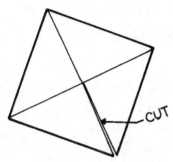

3. Open the paper and cut on one folded line to the center.

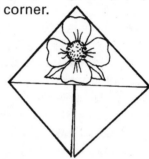

4. Draw and color your insect's habitat on the top half.

5. Neatly print your pyramid poem on the bottom triangle.

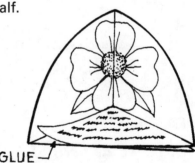

6. Keeping the poem on top, overlap the two sections, and glue.

7. Draw, color, and cut out your insect.

8. Using a needle and thread poke a hole through your insect and suspend it in the center of the pyramid by poking another hole in the peak, leaving a bit of length on the thread and then tying a knot large enough so it will not slip through.

Recipe Poem

Developing Skills
Students will use cooking terms with other nouns, ordinarily not associated with cooking, to write a recipe poem.

Resources/Materials
Resources: cookbooks and recipes

Materials: copies of the activity page, 5" x 7" file cards, chart paper, markers, paper, pencils, and pens

Prewriting
Organize cooperative learning groups of four to six students. Give each group a variety of cookbooks and recipes. Each group selects a recorder. Then, the students browse through the cookbooks to find verbs that apply to cooking. The recorder keeps a list of such terms for the group. Examples: bake, peel, mash, cook, mix, sprinkle, stir, chop, and so on. The students also look for nouns that name measurements often used in cooking—cup, teaspoon, tablespoon, ounce, etc.

Writing
Explain that each student in the group will write a recipe for success at school. The student lists the ingredients and gives directions for success.

Example:

Success at School

Ingredients:
1 teacher
25 students
1 cup of love
2 cups of patience
1/2 cup of understanding
dash of humor
1 tablespoon of silence
sprinkle of homework
1 pint of cheerfulness

Mix teacher and students in a large classroom. Add love, patience, and understanding. Stir in humor, silence, *and a sprinkle of homework. Bake in the classroom for one year. Spread cheerfulness on top and serve warm to everyone.*

Responding
Each student shares his/her recipe for success with the group. Members of the group make suggestions for improving the recipe.

Revising/Editing
Each author may choose to revise his/her poem as suggested by the response group. Then, the student checks spelling.

Postwriting
Each student writes his/her recipe for school success on a copy of the activity page. Put all the recipes in a class book. Then, the author writes his/her recipe on a file card to keep.

Evaluating
The student made two copies of his/her poem in neat handwriting. The student participated in the cooperative learning group.

Extending Writing
Have students collect favorite recipes and write a class cookbook for Mother's Day.

Have students write recipes for a variety of topics: "Fun with My Family," "How to Make Friends," and so on.

Cooking Class *(recipe poem)*

Sensory Poem

Developing Skills
The students will express their feelings in a sensory poem, following a prescribed pattern.

Resources/Materials
Resources: health textbooks and poems about feelings

Materials: chart paper, markers, writing paper, pencils, and copies of the activity page (Mobile Materials: 1 metal coat hanger per student, assorted colors of construction paper, scissors, markers, varying lengths of yarn or ribbon, glue or staples, and a hole punch)

Prewriting
Brainstorm emotions: joy, happiness, pride, excitement, sadness, cheerfulness, anger, loneliness, love, hate, and so on. Record them on a chart to keep. Read the examples of sensory poems below. Write the pattern for the poem on a chart to keep for another session. Then, choose one emotion and write a sensory poem together, line by line.

Pattern:
Line 1: Name an emotion or feeling.
        Finish the line with a color word.
Line 2: Tell what it sounds like.
Line 3: Tell what it smells like.
Line 4: Tell what it tastes like.
Line 5: Tell what it looks like.
Line 6: Tell what it feels like.

Examples:

Anger is red.
It sounds like a fire engine.
It smells like firecrackers.
It tastes like jalapeño peppers.
It looks like jagged flames.
Anger feels like a sharp knife.

Cheerfulness is yellow.
It sounds like a baby's laughter.
It smells like lilies of the valley.
It tastes like pie á la mode.
It looks like a field of sunflowers.
Cheerfulness feels like the warm sun.

Writing
Each student chooses an emotion from the brainstormed list to write a sensory poem following the prescribed pattern.

Responding
Each student reads his/her poem to the members of the peer group. Positive comments are made and suggestions for improving the poem are given.

Revising/Editing
Each author makes the necessary corrections and checks for capitalization and punctuation.

Postwriting
The author follows the directions given on the activity page to construct a mobile to display his/her poem.

Evaluating
The student used appropriate sentences to refer to an emotion. The student followed the directions to make a mobile.

Extending Writing
Have students write definition poems about emotions. See page 20 for the pattern for a definition poem.

Have students write sensory poems about each of the four seasons. Write them on large pieces of poster board and illustrate them with colored markers.

THE FOUR SEASONS

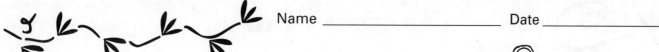

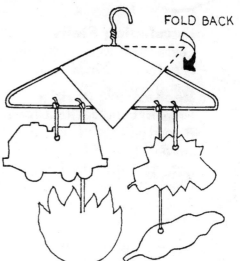

FOLD BACK

Emotions *(sensory poem)*

1. Fold a 9" square of construction paper in half diagonally. Cut on the fold to make two triangles.

2. With a marker, write the first line of your poem in the center of one triangle (point is down). Fold the corners of the triangle over the hanger as shown. Glue or staple the two folded points.

3. Cut and trace the four patterns below on assorted colors of construction paper. Write lines two, three, four, and five, each on a different shape. Cut out.

4. Using the hole punch, make a hole at the top center of each of those four shapes. Attach varying lengths of yarn or ribbon to the shapes and hang them from the bottom of the coat hanger.

5. Write the last line of your poem in the center of the second triangle (point is up this time). Punch a hole in the center of the point. Attach the longest piece of yarn or string and hang it from the center of the coat hanger. The triangle should be hanging below the other shapes.

6. Illustrate the back of each shape with an appropriate picture.

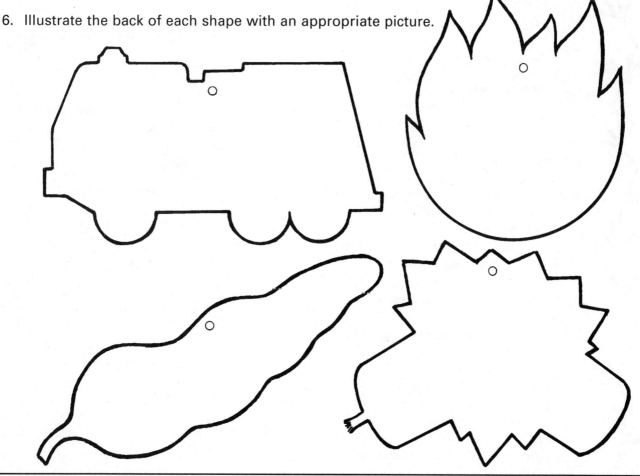

Terse Verse

Developing Skills
Students will write riddles for which the answers are pairs of rhyming words.

Resource/Materials
Resources: Joseph Rosenbloom's *Biggest Riddle Book in the World* and *696 Silly School Jokes & Riddles*; Monika Beisner's *Book of Riddles* by Monika Beisner; and Charles Keller's *Count Draculations: Monster Riddles*, and *Colossal Fossils: Dinosaur Riddles*.

Materials: copies of the activity page, chart paper, markers, paper, pencils, crayons, 9" x 12" white paper, and stapler

Prewriting
Read a variety of riddles from the resources listed above. Then, explain that a special kind of riddle asks a question that is answered with a pair of rhyming words. Example: *What do you call a concise poem?* (a terse verse)

Write the following terse verses on a chart for the class to answer.

What do you call a parakeet that talks?
   a word bird
What do you call an amphibian in the middle of the street? **a road toad**
What do you call a pig that sits on a tree trunk? **a log hog**
What do you call a lamb that cries all day long? **a weepy sheepy**
What do you call a beach for T-Rexes?
   a dinosaur shore
What do you call a colt that eats lunch meat? **a bologna pony**
What do you call it when a hen gets a spanking? **a chicken lickin'**
What do you call a lame turkey?
   a hobbler gobbler

Writing
Each student chooses a particular subject—animals, plants, people—about which to write several terse verses.

Responding
Response teams listen as each student reads his/her riddle. They try to think of a pair of rhyming words for each riddle. They can make suggestions to the author to improve the questions.

Revising/Editing
Authors make necessary revisions to their riddles and check proper usage of capitalization and punctuation. (The two-word answers do not need punctuation.)

Postwriting
The student follows the directions on the activity page to write his/her terse verses.

Evaluating
The student wrote several riddles and two-word rhyming answers. The student made a neat riddle flap booklet with appropriate illustrations.

Extending Writing
Write terse verses about food. Ask permission to share these verses in the school cafeteria on a bulletin board or wall area.

Examples:

What do you call a flighty cucumber?
   a fickle pickle
What do you call a cruel legume?
   a mean bean

The Riddler *(terse verse)*

To make a flap booklet:

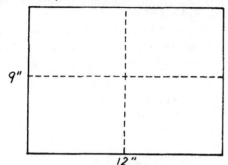

1. Fold a sheet of 9" x 12" white drawing paper in half vertically and horizontally.

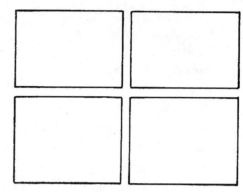

2. Cut on the folded lines.

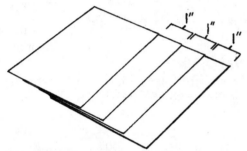

3. Stack the four pages, offsetting each page one inch.

4. Cut the four pages at the top of the bottom sheet.

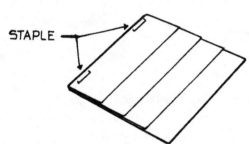

5. Staple the pages at the top.

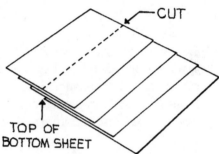

6. On the top sheet write: "Terse Verses" by… (write your name).

7. Write a riddle on the bottom of each page.

8. Lift the flap, write the answer and illustrate it.

Two-Worder

Developing Skills

Students will use facts to write poems with two words per line that relate to spiders. Students will use capitalization and punctuation, following the pattern of the poem.

Resources/Materials

Resources: Michael Chinery's *Spider*, Luise Woelflein's *Spider*, and Christine Back and Barrie Watts' *Spider's Web*

Materials: copies of the activity page, chart paper, markers, tagboard, black construction paper, white thread, colored pom-pons, pipe cleaners, writing paper, and pencils

Prewriting

Give students the opportunity to do research on arachnids, using a variety of materials. Students should keep notes on their findings, using index cards. Explain that they will use the information to write factual two-worders about spiders. Write the example of a two-worder on a chart.

Spectacular Spiders

Shy creatures,
Eat insects,
Spin silk,
Eight eyes,
Hairy bodies,
Sense vibrations,
Lay eggs,
Web builders,
Some bite.

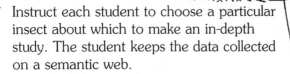

Instruct each student to choose a particular insect about which to make an in-depth study. The student keeps the data collected on a semantic web.

Writing

Students may write about spiders in general as in the example, or they may choose specific spiders for their two-worders.

Examples:

Terrifying Tarantulas   Black Widows

Each line of the poem begins with a capital letter and ends with a comma, except for the last. Students should strive to have six to nine lines in their poems.

Responding

Students meet in peer groups to share their poems about spiders. The response group offers praise for particularly interesting lines. Members may suggest rearranging lines to make a poem flow better. Students check for fact accuracy with the author's research note cards.

Revising/Editing

The author may choose to revise his/her poem according to a response group's suggestions. Then, students check for proper usage of capitalization and punctuation.

Postwriting

The student follows directions on the activity page to make a spider's web and a spider. The student produces a neat copy of his/her two-worder to attach below the web.

Evaluating

The student used facts about spiders to write a two-worder poem. He/she followed directions to complete a spider web and spider. The student produced a neat copy of his/her poem.

Extending Writing

Students may use a Venn diagram to compare two different spiders.

Students write five-paragraph reports about spiders.

Students write haiku poetry about spiders. See page 26 for information on haiku.

Spider Webs *(two-worder)*

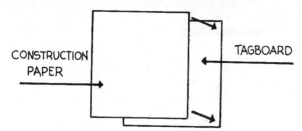

CONSTRUCTION PAPER

TAGBOARD

1. Glue a 9" square of black construction paper onto a 9" square of tagboard, making sure the edges are sealed.

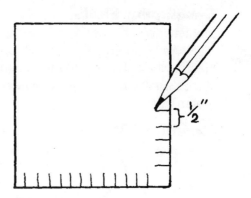

½"

2. Mark the backside of the tagboard at ½" intervals around the four edges.

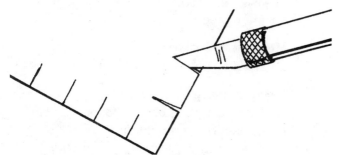

3. Make small cuts at the ½" marks.

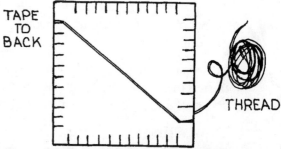

TAPE TO BACK

THREAD

4. Tape the end of a piece of white thread to the back of the square. Then, bring it to the front through a slit, across the center, and out the slit diagonally opposite it.

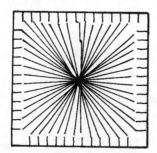

5. Continue until all the strands of the web are completed. Tape the end to the back.

6. Bend four pipe cleaners down to form legs, twisting them in the center.

7. Glue a large pom-pon on top of the legs to make the spider's body.

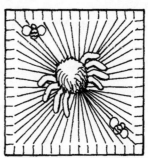

8. Glue the spider to the center of the web. Add cut paper insects caught by the spider, if you wish.

Two-Worder

Developing Skills
Students will use a set of tangrams to make a picture of an object related to Christmas, Hanukkah, or Kwanzaa celebrations. Then, students will write two-worder poems about their pictures.

Resources/Materials
Resources: Clement Moore's poem "A Visit from St. Nicholas," and Aileen Fisher's "Light the Festive Candles," from *The Random House Book of Poetry for Children*, edited by Jack Prelutsky, *It's Christmas* by Jack Prelutsky, Eric Kimmel's *The Chanukkah Guest*, *Hanukkah Money* by Scholem Aleichem, and *Kwanzaa* by A. P. Porter

Materials: copies of the activity page, chart paper, markers, paper, pencils, glue, scissors, and colored construction paper

Prewriting
Read stories and poems about Christmas, Hanukkah, and Kwanzaa to the class. Brainstorm about symbols used in each one of the three celebrations. Write them on chart paper. Then using tangrams, have the students create a symbol of one of the three celebrations. Directions are given on the activity page.

Writing
Write the following examples of two-worder poems on chart paper to share with the class.

Christmas Tree
Green pine,
Lights glow,
Ornaments sparkle,
Garlands, star,
Presents below.

My Dreidle
Spinning top,
Nun, gimmel,
Heh, shin
Gold coins,
Ancient game.

Kwanzaa Celebration
Cultural holiday,
Seven principles,
Black, red,
Green colors,
Heritage shield.

Then, each student writes a two-worder poem about his/her holiday symbol. It does not need to rhyme. Encourage students to write at least four lines.

Responding
Students meet in response groups to share their poems. Participants give authors positive comments and make suggestions for improving poems.

Revising/Editing
Each author makes desired revisions.

Postwriting
Each student glues his/her tangram picture on a sheet of construction paper, allowing room for a neat, clean copy of his/her poem to be placed next to it.

Evaluating
The student used correct information to write a two-worder about a holiday symbol he/she created with tangrams.

Extending Writing
Students write paragraphs about Christmas, Hanukkah, or Kwanzaa.

Make separate class booklets of all the poems for each of the three celebrations.

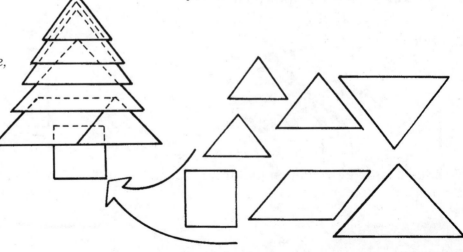

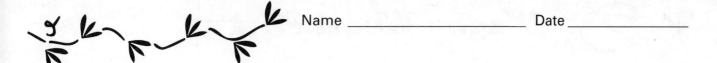

Celebrations *(two-worder)*

To make a tangram picture:

Cut out the square below and cut apart the pieces. Use all seven shapes to make an object described in your poem. Pieces may be turned and flipped. After you have constructed an object, draw a sketch of it to help you remember the placement of the tangram pieces. Then, trace the tangram pieces on construction paper, the color of which is appropriate for your object. Glue all the pieces on a large sheet of construction paper, allowing room for you to place a copy of your poem beside or below the object.

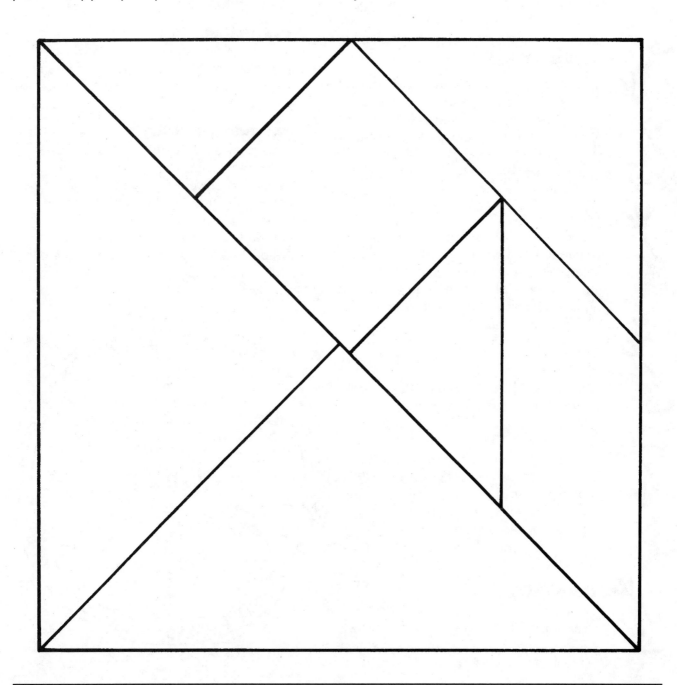

Wagon Wheel Poetry

Developing Skills

Students will write a wagon wheel poem about the westward expansion of the United States. Although this lesson is about a specific topic, wagon wheel poetry can be written about any subject.

Resources/Materials

Resources: Ellen Levine's *If You Traveled West in a Covered Wagon*, Russell Freedman's *Children of the Wild West*, and Pam Conrad's *Prairie Visions: The Life and Times of Solomon Butcher*, and also *Prairie Songs*, reference books, and social studies texts

Materials: two copies of the activity page for each student, chart paper, markers, writing paper, and pencils. Materials for making a diorama: shoe box per student, construction paper (self-adhesive paper optional), markers, transparent tape, crayons, scissors, and glue

Prewriting

After sufficient study about the westward expansion of the United States, brainstorm nouns about the movement and write them on chart paper. Examples: covered wagon, prairie, Homestead Act, gold rush, railroad, Oregon Trail, Santa Fe Trail, sod house, wagon train, Indians, and frontier.

Writing

Students write their rough drafts on copies of the activity page. Tell them to write "Westward Expansion" in the center of the wagon wheel. Then, instruct them to write six nouns that refer to the topic on the spokes of the wheels. They may use the words generated in the prewriting activity. Next, they write phrases or sentences containing some of those nouns on the outer rims of the wheels. Encourage them to use adjectives.

Responding

Each author shares his/her rough draft with a peer group. Students should verify any facts called into question. Peers make suggestions for writing more picturesque phrases.

Revising/Editing

The student revises his/her poem and checks for correct capitalization, punctuation, and spelling.

Postwriting

Each student copies his/her poem on a new copy of the wagon wheel and cuts it out. Then, the student follows the directions on the activity page for making a diorama depicting the westward expansion movement.

Evaluating

The student composed a wagon wheel poem and produced a neat copy. He/she followed directions for making a diorama to display the poem.

Extending Writing

Have students write wagon wheel poems about other topics concerning the westward expansion movement. Examples: *pioneers, the Plains Indians, the California gold rush, cowboys, the transcontinental railroad.* They can use poems about fictional accounts of the times in place of writing book reports.

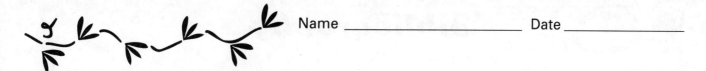

Name _____   Date _____

Westward, Ho! *(wagon wheel poetry)*

To make a diorama:

Cover the outside of a shoe box with construction paper (or self-adhesive paper). Use construction paper, crayons, and markers to create a scene inside the box that depicts the westward expansion movement. Tape the copy of the wagon wheel poem on the front of the diorama as shown.

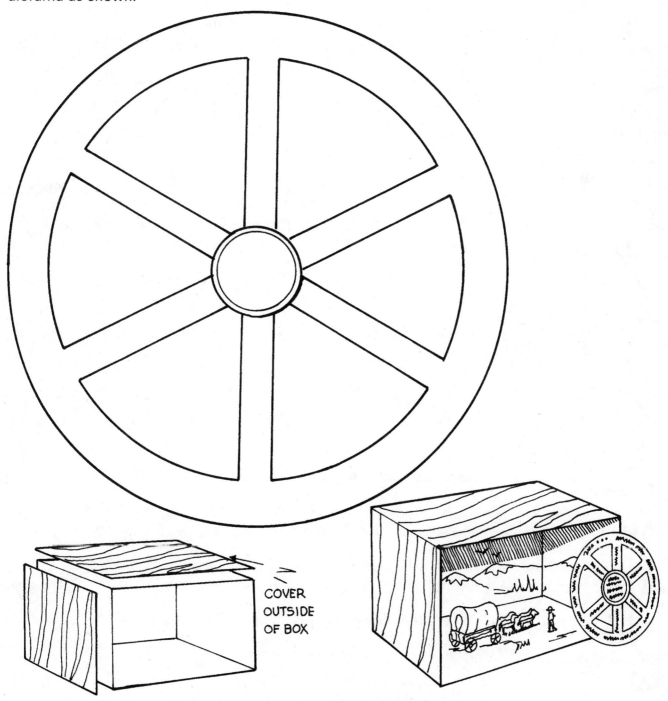

COVER
OUTSIDE
OF BOX

Bibliography

Adolff, Arnold, ed. *I am the Darker Brother: An Anthology of Modern Poems by Black Americans*, New York: Aladdin, 1968.

Atwood, Ann. *My Own Rhythm,* New York: Charles Scribner's Sons, 1973.

_____. *Haiku-vision,* New York: Charles Scribner's Sons, 1977.

Benet, Rosemary and Stephen Vincent. *Book of Americans*, New York: Holt, Rinehart, and Winston, 1961.

Ciardi, John. *Hopeful Trout and Other Limericks*, Boston: Houghton Mifflin, 1989.

Dickinson, Emily. *I'm Nobody! Who Are You? Poems of Emily Dickinson for Young People*, Owings Mills, Maryland: Stemmer House, 1978.

Frost, Robert, *Swinger of Birches: Poems of Robert Frost for Young Children*, Owings Mills, Maryland: Stemmer House, 1982.

Giovanni, Nikki. *Spin A Soft Black Song,* New York: Farrar, Straus, Giroux, 1985.

Hall, Donald, ed. *The Oxford Book of Children's Verse in America*, London: Oxford University Press, 1985.

Kennedy, X.J. and Dorothy M. *Knock at a Star: A Child's Introduction to Poetry*, Boston: Little, Brown and Company, 1982.

Koch, Kenneth. *Wishes, Lies, and Dreams*, New York: Perennial Bilrary, Harper and Row, 1970.

Nash, Ogden. *Custard and Company*, Boston: Little, Brown and Company, 1980.

Prelutsky, Jack, ed. *The Random House of Poetry for Children*, New York: Random House, 1983.

_____ . *New Kid on the Block*, New York: William Morrow, 1984.

Rosen, Michael, ed. *Kingfisher Book of Children's Poetry*, (New York: Chambers Kingfisher Graham Publishers, 1993.

Sandburg, Carl. Edited by Lee Bennet Hopkins. *Rainbows Are Made*, Orlando: Harcourt Brace Jovanovich, 1982.

Silverstein, Shel. *Where the Sidewalk Ends*, New York: Harper and Row, 1974.

_____ . *A Light in the Attic*, New York: Harper and Row, 1981.